GIMME FIVE

Poems
by
Philip Dacey

BLUE LIGHT PRESS ◆ 1ST WORLD PUBLISHING

1ST WORLD
PUBLISHING

SAN FRANCISCO ◆ FAIRFIELD ◆ DELHI

GIMME FIVE

BLUE LIGHT PRESS
www.bluelightpress.com
Email: bluelightpress@aol.com

Book Design:
Melanie Gendron

Cover Art:
"Five Cosmic Petals" by Melanie Gendron

Author Photograph:
Robert Medina

GIMME FIVE website:
www.philipdacey.com

FIRST EDITION

LCCN: 2013932519

ISBN: 978-1-4218-8661-9

In biology the number 5 crops up more than its share of times. Practically all land vertebrates have five fingers and five toes on each limb. Even the horse has five: its hoof is really an enlarged fingernail. Most modern starfish have five arms. Fossil remains indicate starfish that aren't five-armed have all died out.

—Scot Morris, *Omni* magazine

Among the rain
and lights
I saw the figure 5
in gold
on a red
firetruck . . .

—William Carlos Williams, "The Great Figure"

Five is
the human soul.

—Schiller, *Piccolomini*

Oblivious to the food in restaurants, choreographer
Doris Humphrey always ordered the fifth item on the menu.

—Barbara Pollack, *Dance Is a Moment*

For every breath, five heartbeats.

—Bryan Aubrey, "Supernatural Love"

ACKNOWLEDGEMENTS

Poems in this collection have appeared in the following periodicals, chapbooks, and anthologies: *Alkali Flats, Back Door, Big City Lit, Blue Earth Review, The Chaffin Journal, Chiron Review, Chouteau Review, Coming Together: Love Poems* (Pflaum,1975), *Comstock Review, The Condom Poems* (Ox Head Press, 1979), *The Condom Poems 2* (Spoon River Poetry Press, 1989), *Cortland Review, The Darfur Anthology* (Elgin Community College, 2007), *The Eleventh Muse, English Journal, Fish Sweet Giraffe the Lion Snake and Owl* (Back Door, 1970), *Fives* (Spoon River Poetry Press, 1984), *Four Nudes* (Morgan Press, 1971), *Free Lunch, Getting It On: A Condom Reader* (Soho Press, 1999), *The Greenfield Review, Green Hills Literary Lantern, Gumball Poetry, Hampden-Sydney Poetry Review, Hurakan: A Journal of Contemporary Literature, Innisfree Poetry Journal, The Journal, Kansas Quarterly, Lake Street Review, Laurel Review, Literary Review, Mobius: The Poetry Magazine, Mr. Five-by-Five* (Pudding House Publications, 2005), *Movieworks: Stories and Poems About Movies* (Little Theatre Press, 1990), *New York Times, North Coast Review, North Stone Review, Outerbridge, Paintbrush, Poet Lore, Poetry East, Poetry Midwest, Poetry Northwest, Quarterly West, Red Booth Review, Red Cedar Review, Red River Review, The Same, Seems, Skidrow Penthouse, Southern Poetry Review, Sou'wester, Spectrum: The Richmond Tri-Annual Review, Spoon River Poetry Quarterly, Studio One, Three Shades of Green: Poems of Fatherhood* (Snark Publishing, 2006), *Token Entry: Poems of the New York City Subway* (Small's Press, 2012, including a cd with animation by Jack Feldstein of "Subway Services"), *Umbrella, Visions, The Western Journal of Medicine, Zone 3.*

AUTHOR'S NOTE

Since 1967, when my poetry began appearing in print, I have often though not exclusively written what I call 5x5 poems—my first published poem was such a one—i. e., poems of five stanzas of five lines each, a structure suggested in part, as I recall, by some of James Dickey's early work. This collection brings together a selection of those that have appeared in periodicals, chapbooks, and anthologies but not yet been included in any of my full-length books. Despite the handful of opening epigraphs about the number 5 that might suggest otherwise and which I include just for the record, I make no case for the significance of what seems to me a fundamentally arbitrary form—or format—beyond testifying that for me it has acted like a sculptor's standard armature upon which he or she can build up an unlimited variety of shapes and configurations. I also wish to thank David Pichaske for his early support of my "fives."

for Sorcha

in welcome

PRONOUNCING HER NAME

Rhyme it with Portia. Sorcha.
No cha-cha-cha,
though she's a reason to dance.
Sound the "c" and "h" of chanteuse—
you should hear her sing already—

or chandelier—her Irish name
means "light"—or champagne—
celebrate this newborn.
Shall she shine? She shall.
Now hush. Shh. She sleeps.

In her dream, the susurrus
of the Floridian shore—Sorshore—
the shushing around her small feet
a pressure to erode harsh
old Irish, where the "c" and "h"

harden to a "k," as in the chasm
she crossed to get here; Chronos,
this Time she has entered with us;
chorus, as with many voices
raised in praise; or even chlorophyll,

the green of beginnings.
For now she has brought softness
to the Irish language
and to us—see Sorcha
in her first chemise.

TABLE OF CONTENTS

Dedication: Pronouncing Her Name

ARRIVING LATE FOR A MOVIE

If you miss the beginning,
you miss the end.
The end
is in the beginning.
There are signs

at the very start
as to what the final
scene will mean.
The deathbed that rides
off into the sunset

could be comic or not,
depending on the light
modelling the baby's
emerging head
as the credits begin.

And the fire
in the middle, the beginning
lost, becomes
mere calories,
something to read by,

though the flames
lick the root of the tongue.
Coming in late, you tread
on toes and spill
a handful, a mouthful.

ON TRIAL IN A DREAM, HE IS ASKED, "WHERE IS THE ISLAND OF JAVA?"

"Like umbrellas in Java."
—Wallace Stevens

The island of Java is in the Black Sea,
a few leagues from the Isthmus of Cream.
It broke off long ago from Havana
and is where I committed the act
now considered a crime.

Is it lost, the island of Java?
Am I accused of a theft?
That Java, the island of islands,
should be missing—imagine!
If Java's not safe, then what is?

It's true I loved Java,
but not to possess it.
Search all of my islands
in all of my waters,
you'll find nothing but dregs.

Once I was there, or dreamed so,
the women of Java as dark as its drink,
which was strong, a capital sentence.
Did it madden my blood?
Each question's an island, including

the question stirred into the brew
as I ask it: is it true
all questions boil down to this one
that arraigns me? Really, I don't have a
clue. Where, where, is the island of Java?

ALIEN

In *Starman*, Jeff Bridges
plays an alien trying to play,
during his brief stay here, a human,
whose body he has restored to life
and entered. As creatures also

attempting to be human,
we identify with the alien,
don't understand the humans
anymore than he—it—does, are threatened
by their strange, even murderous, ways.

Our road trip from Wisconsin
to Arizona allowed us time
to learn to speak and therefore
get ourselves into trouble.
Even though we know the rescue ship

to bring us to our star is on its way,
we can't help holding in our mouth
as long as possible the bite of apple pie
in the diner, our first taste of Earth.
Nor can we keep from falling in love

with the woman who loved the body we're in
before we were in it. We are not sure
as we lift off whether we are
going home or leaving it.
It's a human confusion.

TWO YEARS IN ONE

In one 1939, Germany
invaded Poland; in the other,
I was born. My fingers
curled open; Pavel's
curled shut. I marched

in circles to the tune
of my mother's breasts
and saluted myself
without knowing it.
I was occupied, all right,

the days knew me
from border to border.
The ghost of my Polish
great-grandmother stitched
a thread between me

and a land where smoke
wrote names in the sky.
Swaddled by a headline,
I slept through one
death after another

and woke up refreshed.
Now I think of booties
and boots, blue and black,
feet struggling
for a place on the earth.

NOT CORRECTING HIS NAME MISSPELLED
ON THE MAILING LABEL

Daley. I'm that one, too,
or ought to be. Daily.
Diurnal. To die earnestly
into the hour, the urn shaped
like a woman's body

that turns over and over,
lover to lover,
tireless hole
into which the universe
rushes, dallying. Dali

at work, melting time.
Quotidian, too,
no tedium, quite,
all queynt and caper. Once,

for months, I was Decay.
The mail got to me, the vowels
dancing their round.
I've never been Decay since.
Now I want to be Cyaed,

a Welsh verse form
impossible to pronounce,
a near-forgotten
arrangement of sounds
some few mouths can enjoy.

THE FIVE SENSES: A BESTIARY

the small dog of the nose
rummaging in the wind
a stray
he never gets
anything substantial

mouth
belly of a little
leviathan with a taste
for Jonah
who can no longer be found

the ears a pair of birds
they want to lift
the head off
and fly it back
to its home star

the curled brown bears
of the eyes
when they dislike what they see
they say it is winter
and sleep in a cave

fingers a tangle
of snakes one rears up
from the ground
and points at you saying
we would nest in your hair

HANDS

The hands of Anderson's
character fluttered
into boys' hair.
Some hands crawl
all the way home

to discover the wrist is gone.
Hands rising into the air
like birds
to be shot down.
The green hand around the heart.

The hand years
in pockets,
its fingers blinded
the day of exit.
The hand meaning

to thrill high
above the crowd
but forgetting its act.
Hands recurring
in the dreams of snakes.

All the hands
ascended to a
heaven of hands,
all of them applauding
forever.

MAIL

The best-class mail
is secret, arriving
at all hours
to change your life,
though you know nothing of it.

And there is the mail
written in code
in your own hand.
You spend years
trying to remember the key.

Some mail gets carried
miles on the back of an animal.
He comes to your doorstep.
He reads it to you.
You go down on all fours.

All mail, whether it says so
or not, is postage-due,
and some of it
returns to you marked
"Sender unknown."

When mail stops arriving,
you begin folding yourself up.
You look for some place
to insert yourself
that will take you away.

MARGINAL EXISTENCE

Here in this white space
we can have a party.
What book is this?
Without us,
the text would bleed

into oblivion.
Do you hear a spine
cracking?
Right now,
someone is making

marginal comments
on us.
Does it tickle?
Does it wound?
We're cornered

and numbered
but we go up
and down
and all around.
If this is poverty,

no one can say
where we end
and what's written
between the lines
begins.

FIRST FIRE OF THE YEAR

Snow recessive like defeated troops.
Paper, cardboard, sticks, logs,
the four corners of the foundation of fire.
Stones as precise around a firepit
as kohl around an eye.

Match, great teacher.
Watch its lessons spread
and change lives.
Flames lift their hands and sing
hallelujah.

Pride collapses upon itself
with a little shower of sparks.
Red thoughts return to the dead in space.
Wood can spit anger like people,
nature all blowtorch and hiss.

This wood worked so hard and long
to arrive here so rich,
and now in minutes, penury, less than penury.
In this school, ash
makes the best valedictorian.

The dream of smoke
is to cling to clothes,
to go indoors
and live for days deep
in soft fibers.

BEYOND THE PALE

"The Pale refers to the English occupiers' garrisons in Ireland."
—*Dictionary of Word Origins*

I like it here.
Those in the Pale
are occupiers;
I'm at home
on the outside.

What's beyond the Pale
is freedom from the walls
that keep the insiders
in and allow us out here
to encircle them all.

You're beyond the Pale, aren't you?
That's why you listen.
You recognize this voice
as similar to your own,
its silent spaces.

Some out here weaken, imagine
an easier life inside. I confess
to such moments, but then I think
of the crowding there
and the view from here:

looking up, those in the Pale
see only the high sides
of the fortress and a square sky;
out here we measure our lives
by the distant horizon.

HISTORY

"History happens behind our backs."
—Jonathan Jones, *Manchester Guardian*

Don't turn around.
Or if you do, turn
slowly. Or use a mirror
to look behind you.
It's safer that way.

In any case, the world
back there is a book
you'll never read.
That breeze on your neck?
Someone else is turning the pages.

How's your backside looking?
That's what counts.
Not you coming towards
but you going away.
Our butts are showing

through the centuries.
If you could only notice
what you're not noticing,
you'd walk backwards
into your history.

In the prehistoric meantime,
enjoy what's in front,
what will never fit,
darkened and shelved,
on any page.

PRAYING MANTISES, 1963

I'd be reading, late at night,
the peace of the Nigerian bush
a dark surround,
my kerosene lamp
the center of the world,

when suddenly through the open window
they'd come whirring, hot for light,
and find me in the way.
Their impact and tangled thrashing in my hair
shocked me into my own thrashing:

I clawed them free and threw them to the floor,
where my shoe was executioner.
Not even their large eyes could stop me.
Then ants came up through cracks in the floor
to dismantle the mantises

and drag their parts back down into the dark
so that shortly after their deaths
the crime scene was as clean
as my conscience.
Now, decades later, the dead insects return.

They sit at the foot of the bed
or on the arm of a chair.
Though small, the delicate green creatures
cast a great shadow,
which surrounds and includes me.

IN THE SUMMER OF 1993, HE DISCOVERS IN HIS MEDICINE CHEST A COMPLIMENTARY BOXED BAR OF SOAP HE ACQUIRED IN THE PALACE HOTEL, BELGRADE, DURING HIS 1988 TENURE IN YUGOSLAVIA AS A FULBRIGHT FELLOW

Oh, I am returning this, thanks,
to you, for your coming clean,
not for your cleansing, no, not that,
but for the washing from your hands
of those stubborn stains I have been

reading about with disbelief, my memories
of Sarajevo including no one sufficiently
astonished then—certainly not me—
at the peacefulness of your most
rainbowed and open city, like

a feast spread out for all comers
at the foot of the hills. So I return
this soap to you intact—the bar, that is,
not you, who are barely intact. Its suds will rise
and take you by the hand, provided you first

remove all your clothing and stand
in the River Drina or Sava or Danube,
as if for a baptism, before letting yourself
fall trustingly backwards into the arms
of the water like an actor warming up

with his partner for a performance of
Waiting for Godot by the Mostar Players.
Meanwhile, without this bar, I will of course
be getting dirty here rehearsing
my own history in my own place.

NOVEMBER, 2000

After the election,
the English language,
which had taken such a beating,
flew to the Virgin Islands
for a rest.

It stuck its feet
into the Caribbean
and kept its mouth shut,
listening to the sibilance
of the waves, the crying

of the seagulls
off St. Croix.
The legacy upon which
millions depended
took those sounds

deep into itself,
rebuilding consonants
and vowels
from scratch.
And at night

it stayed out on the beach,
looking up at the great O
of the moon, like the beginning
of a sentence
spoken from the heart.

THE PRESIDENT SAVES FACE

At night I keep it in
a jar
among emollients.
It will grow
with interest.

Give yours
that I might save mine.
I see the beautiful
blank oval
above your collarbone

as purest love.
Which came first,
the mirror or the face?
Hot towels
often cover mine,

steaming with authority.
I would be all face,
the world and you
all mirror.
Let's face it,

even God gave his
on the cross
to save mine.
I thank you
from the bottom of my face.

PUBLIC RADIO

In a dream, the radio announcer
introduces the next piece as
A Tissue of Liars
and I awaken into my own tissue,
one of the liars, no doubt.

The music must have been
a classical composition,
something diaphanous,
a touch of Debussy, perhaps,
for the bodies of those

who have told so many lies
are transparent,
as thin as beaten gold,
thinner: the liars are hanging
from absolutely nothing

like a curtain, a long, flowing
invention whipped
to a chiffon that's almost
pure absence itself, like any life
any day of the week.

The sun lies about light
and we welcome the lie.
Wipe away your tears
with this tissue, although it will tear
easily, and that's the truth.

THE CONDOM

He could put it on
with one hand
and in a single
motion so smooth
his woman said

he ought to do that
for a living. People
would pay to see
that, she said.
So he practiced

before the mirror
a whole year
before hitting the
county-fair circuit
where, she was right,

he made enough
to retire on
and after that just
lay around thinking
of a comeback,

of escaping handcuffed
from an oversized one,
a Houdini risking
his life time and again
inside an airtight skin.

THE CONDOM'S NIGHTMARE

I grow up to be
a great
German dirigible.
I hover
in the night sky

above Dusseldorf,
Weimar,
Cologne,
the pride of the Vaterland,
my belly and sides

spotlit from below.
Atop yellow columns, I look
like an architrave
proclaiming my name:
the Hindenburg.

And then, always,
without warning,
I burst into flames.
Suddenly
I am a fiery skeleton.

Burning gobs of my flesh
fall to the platz
below. People scatter,
screaming. I wake up
in a sweat that leaks.

MEN-STRUAL

"Havelock Ellis suggested that males possess some traces of a rudimentary menstrual cycle."

—*Encyclopedia of Victorian Sexuality*

What was I to make
of the spot of blood
on my jock strap?
Tennis
is no contact sport

and I had just had
my yearly checkup. I was
100%.
But there it was,
a red period at the end

of a sentence I couldn't read.
Twenty-eight days later,
the same period, the sentence
becoming clearer.   I loved
the woman I lived with,

but now I began to dream
of rags, of the poverty
of simple thoughts,
and of rich
Tiresias,

condemned to the beauty
of a moon with no side
in shadow, somewhere
a secret sun,
or a light within.

HE RECEIVES IN THE MAIL AN INVITATION
TO JOIN O.W.L, THE OLD WOMEN'S LEAGUE

I'm putting on a long grey wig.
I'm getting heavy stockings that sag.
I'll be my grandmother,
a little dumpy, and call
young people "dearie."

I can be crazy
with impunity, say
whatever I want.
I'll pity old men
with their vacant stares,

their lost directions,
as I wear the word "crone"
like a badge.
And I'll visit gravesites,
lay down flowers, real ones,

lay myself down, the real me.
Passersby will wonder,
"Poor old woman, she must have lost
a son, or a dear husband,"
but the graves will be those

of strangers, my sisters.
Lying there, impersonating
someone dead, I'll hoot
and hoot, as if I'd just heard
a good one.

THE NUDE

She is my island.
The breasts are full of stories.
Her feet grow
as big as pans.
She is my kitchen

where beans cook.
I can take her apart
and lose pieces of her.
When I sleep next to her
I am amazed

how she is all one.
Birds settle on her limbs
and peck at my eyes.
Knees the skullcaps of saints,
elbows the bends of the road

I race up on into mountains,
hips saltlicks for ghost-animals.
Who better to swill
than this enormous cool drink?
By lifting a mere finger,

she has brought back the tradition
of the grand hotel.
At night, the trains of her body
rush past the burning stations
of her soul.

THE RACING FORM

"I have been partial to women jockeys ever since the time Robyn
C. Smith brought a filly named Bel Sheba around seven furlongs at
Saratoga, her hair let loose from under her cap and streaming and I
thought if I touched it I would burn my hand."

—Gary Gildner

And the cap flies off
and then the blouse,
silk rainbow
the wind balloons,
then breeches, boots,

and she's left with
only underthings,
still riding hard,
the whip falls again
and again to the flank

of her naked horse,
and now the pink
top flutters away
and the bottoms tear
easily and ride the air.

O, it is too late
to bet on her!
I watch, through tears,
her body move
with her mount's and cheer

against myself, the wad
I put down on the field.
As she wins, her whip
turns into a snake
wearing the colors of God.

MOVIE KISSES

Technicians surround us,
measuring the distance
from our lips to the lens.
We've practiced this,
we're good at it.

If I put my hand
here and she puts hers
there and our heads tilt
like so, we look the way
you think you'd look

in the same situation,
but this way hurts.
It hurts because it isn't true.
We're actors aching
to release each other,

to escape the light
in our faces that blinds
us for the sake
of romantic shadows and
the perfect picture of love.

Leaving the set at night,
we go our separate ways,
glad to avoid the close
company until tomorrow
when the camera rolls again.

SWEARING OFF MOVIES,
SWEARING OFF WOMEN

I'm tempted
to think they're the same.
The glamour,
and larger than life.
And afterwards thoughts

of the sucker's game.
God's trick of sex,
Hollywood's of
celluloid thanks
to the persistence of vision.

The previews show
the hottest scenes, the freest
flights through air.
I'll make the movie of my life
an endless run of previews.

Of course, I admit there are
classics I would not want
to have missed—the hero
lost, then kissed—
and that I'm to blame

for confusing the two,
out of fear: even now
I remember her embracing
Dolby sound, and the popcorn,
my hand fishing deeper and deeper.

TAKE NO PRISONERS

The mountain range looms
and I must cross it.
I'd like to take you with me
but I know the weather there,
the needs in the pass.

Men have died taking
too much with them,
their bones found under the bones
of their burdens
in the spring.

Therefore, Love,
in contravention
of the agreements,
I must shoot you dead to me.
Coming this far, we have seen

our shadows mix
behind us. Who was holding
whom? Let the sun here
in the valley witness
I acknowledge my guilt.

No doubt when I reach
the other side, I
shall discover I am
carrying the burden
of your absence.

NYCB

"No one should have to choose between a baby and a Balanchine ballet."
—Suzanne Farrell

"...perfection of the life or of the work..."
—Yeats

One day it's baby,
the next it's ballet.
Can't I dance in the delivery room,
lie spread-legged on stage?
So many false dichotomies:

live or die,
truth or consequences.
I ask my husband's opinion,
watch for the crowning
of an answer, but his words

only dance away.
My rehearsal mirror doubles me;
I'll do one in each world.
At the barre, I pretend
my exercises were invented

by Lamaze. Didn't the baby
spring from a pas de deux?
In a dream, Mr. B.
wears a surgical mask
and extracts from me

a Stravinsky score.
What is a nursery
but backstage, all the ballerinas
and their partners
warming up?

THE LOVERS

It is exactly right
the way we hold hands.
Animals could not
do it better.
The grip

is not unlike wrestlers'
or a couple's
at a ledge, one
hanging over. No,
we don't sit so

melodramatically, but we aren't
settled either.
Our hands are
an African plain
small beasts

run over.
There's always
something doing.
As harmless as a helicopter-
safari, perhaps,

or something darker
rushing from the horizon.
See how each hand
keeps up with the other,
exchanging looks!

KEATS AT BEDTIME

I'm showing off the recent
acquisition of "To Autumn"
by my brain and heart, reciting
face to face, our heads on pillows,
my voice gone Brit-plummy.

Now in our harvest years,
we've just harvested
each other, her recent sounds
"treble soft," mine more
"loud bleat," and she's sleepy

but encouraging of this
second performance or encore.
My roving hand underscores
"bosom-friend" and "ripeness,"
"touch" and "hair soft-lifted."

We know we are "the next swath"
the hook spares, and our "twined
flowers" are children and friends,
certain places, the daily round.
With our own "gathering swallows"

circling near, casting shadows
like thoughts weighted
toward winter, we burrow
deeper, the words like snow falling
on eyelashes as her eyes close.

VOCABULARY

for Bruce Boerner

In front of the electrican,
I casually use the word "ambience,"
and he comes back later to ask me
about its spelling, meaning,
exactly how to say it.

He better than anyone
knows the charge of the right word
in the right place, the shock
of the new crackling
through the air.

The next time I see him he stops
to say he likes the ambience
in my office, and we both smile,
knowing it isn't that ambience he likes
but the ambience of his current word.

I take comfort in knowing
there's a poet making the connections
where I work. He must love to say
"wattage" and "volt," as palpably beautiful
in his mouth as the tools slung

at his waist. Now I choose carefully
what I say in front of him, words like
"louche," "chiasmus," "sprezzatura,"
whatever will create sparks,
start a fire.

BIBLIOPHILIA

Proud book-rat,
my tail, like a ribbony
marker, giving me away,
the cover pulled down
cozily over me,

blanket,
coffin-lid,
hatch on my ship.
Sing hand-heft, spine-crack,
dog-ear. Page

after page in waves,
conducted by a finger.
Riffle-music. Friends
dumbly voluble, their
solid shoulders on my shelf.

May I carry yours home after school?
Dangled by a strap around them.
The guts of a satchel
spilled on the dining-room table.
The valley of one opened,

cleavage of intelligence,
two mounds of mother-language.
In the flames of those
afraid of it, it can burn,
its power airborne.

PEN IN HAND

Of all the possible names—
poet, writer, versifier, artist—
I prefer scribbler.
Nothing claimed. How a child writes
before she knows how to write.

Pure gesture.
The hand dancing
just to be dancing.
Each scribbleprint
as good as a fingerprint,

but sometimes even I can't read
what I've written. The words—
are those really words?—exist
on the far edge of penmanship:
the ghost of Sr. Felicitas,

who leaned over my desk
and guided my loops and tails,
shakes her head and prays for me,
her wimple an inviting white page.
Noodling jazz musician,

I scribble my way forward
like one in a labyrinth
until Death writes my name
in his book, he of the most perfect
and beautiful cursive.

HOMAGE TO JOHN ASHBERY

We hang an air freshener
in our brains,
let it work its way out to the fingertips
that touch language
and hoist it into place.

Not so much mint or lemon
as newly minted
in the cave or on cleared ground
(for eating, recreating)
in front of the cave.

Familiar words strange now,
with odd protuberances
and little dents.
To take notice anew
is to remember the chainsaw-like

danger of language. To build
or destroy. Whose finger's that
in the dirt? Lay your tongue lightly
athwart the tasty metal of syllables
lest in the cold your skin stick.

Such a serious playground,
you can turn its pages.
Oh, slide down into the arms
of your condition, brightly lit
in the nighttime park.

HIS LIFE WITH POETRY

Call it a spring,
the way it appeared,
uncalled by me.
Under my feet. The ground
beginning to move. I drank,

shaped the water
with my hands
as it shaped me
when I bent to it.
My joke now is

I'm the chief executive officer
of a largescale waterworks
built on that spot.
I cultivated the gift
of water, dug, cleared away,

so that it could run free
into a system of pipes and canals,
through complicated machines.
The neighborhood's become industrial.
Still, I like to imagine,

somewhere at the center
of it all, in a secret courtyard,
the original spring,
like an innocent girl,
purls and purls.

SHOEHORN

I hadn't used one in years,
had slipped into and out of
this and that without needing help,
but because the new pair of loafers
snugged at the heel I dug out

an old, silver—aluminum, I guess—
shoehorn from the bottom of a drawer
and as if for the first time,
like a shoehorn virgin, inserted it
between shoe and socked heel,

the movement and feel
silky—no, beyond silky,
like that of slipping one's body
into a body of water, then out of it,
letting the water heal.

And now I'm thinking of other shoehorns,
how a word slides between
us and the thing it names
before that word lifts into silence,
leaving us with the thing itself.

And isn't this poem a shoehorn,
the way it has slipped in here between
you and me in order to bring us
closer together when it withdraws,
as it does now, at the end of this line?

AGAINST THE WORD "SPIRITUAL"

I see it laboring beside the road,
then setting down its burden
of meanings that have accumulated
over time on its back,
a great black bag of them,

each weighted by someone's
hopes and desires.
Like a refugee from a war zone,
the word needs to rest awhile.
It needs a great silence

to form around it,
a silence in which it can
renew itself. Let it sleep,
years even, foetal,
and dream of a new body

whose vowels and consonants
know only buoyancy, no drag,
no hands grasping at it.
But for now, have pity on
this exhausted figure of sound,

which has been driven so far
from its root, from "breath,"
it has almost none left.
There is nothing spiritual
about the word "spiritual."

THE PASSWORD

for Ezra

He tells me his password is
"languageismycopilot,"
and I imagine him
handing off the controls
to consonants and vowels,

both he and they wearing goggles,
the cockpit of course open
to the rushing air,
long bright scarves
around his neck and the neck

of aerodynamic syllable
after aerodynamic syllable,
with their lift and tilt
leaving in the blue a trail that forms
a compound-complex sentence.

Sometimes he instructs his copilot,
and sometimes his copilot instructs him.
The way through the sky
is lined like the ruled paper
he wrote on as a child.

For his copilot, no God,
Whose flight log is a series
of disasters; rather,
this partner who sings,
this dictionary with wings.

ANYWHO

I want to name a book *Anywho*,
to honor my father,
the title-word one of his rare
plays on language, along with,
"It shows to go you."

My father's anywhere
right now, the dead
always nowhere
to be seen except
everywhere,

a kind of hoo-doo,
a hoo-ha of absence.
For anywho
is everywho
somehow,

as my father knew,
though every who is ever new. Wow.
Which who are you? Do you coo?
Anyhow, it's all
a bunch of hooey (his word, too),

for who can know the ways—
the how and why—
of any who?
Nobody no how.
It shows to go you.

HER FINGERS

Watching my fingers fly
over the keyboard of my computer,
I, who was thrown out of my high school
typing class for typing faster than
the teacher and not needing the course,

think of my mother in the nursing home,
her hands crippled with arthritis,
and the speed with which they used to fly
over the keyboard of her Underwood
at work, a secretarial speed

maintained also at home when she sat
at the dining room table and typed
letter after letter to friends and relatives
all over the country and in Ireland
as I stood by and watched, in awe,

the digital blur in front of me
that was accompanied by a great clatter
out of which word after word leaped
onto the rolling paper, and now I know
I have my mother's hands and fingers,

their dance on the tops of letters,
like a pair of tap-dancing feet
or bare ones on hot coals,
getting everything said
before the soles burn up.

HAMMER

I hear through the wall of my apartment
the workman next door hammer
against my neighbor's wall in perfect time
to the andante movement of Bach's
first violin concerto in A minor.

A regular at Juilliard, I sit surprised
to be attending a kind of hybrid
concert in my own living room,
half compact disk, half muscled
laborer. Has he heard the Master

coming through the back-to-back bricks
and decided to show his appreciation
in the best way he knows, his arm
like that of a conductor
swinging a heavy baton?

The two form a formidable duo:
Bach the workmanlike musician
and the workman as part-time musician;
Bach, who knew the hammer
of the hammerklavier, and the workman,

who knows how to sustain a good
working rhythm. And now, wanting
to participate in the music-making
and enlarge the duo to a trio, I begin
hammering out these lines.

A PAGE TURNER AT JUILLIARD

I stand and sit back down
and stand and sit back down
while the pianist sits throughout.
I give the audience an opportunity
to practice the art of erasure.

When the music earthquakes
through my body,
I must not show it
but stay upright, hands folded in my lap,
a picture of respectability.

Only my eyes move
as I follow the score,
a predator watching its prey,
though my pounce at the right moment
must be in slow motion.

Or say my hand could be that
of a lover the way, up again,
I arch forward and across
to pull down the corner
of the score so tenderly.

Our heads nearly touching,
I am the priest
hearing confession.
When the pianist admits everything,
I cannot applaud.

AHOY

When the ship goes down, I'll cling
to the desk from my father,
the typewriter from my mother.
They'll be my joint life-raft.
After so many moves, these remain,

always making the final cut,
the one a gift to me in high school
from him who didn't finish grade school,
the other what I watched my mother pound
all through my childhood.

Now one's on top of the other,
my mother on top of my father,
between them the glass plate protecting
the mahogany finish and still,
after decades, impossibly

unbroken, unchipped.
Two icons for a writer,
for a loved son. So when the ship
goes down, I'll cling to them both
in the rough seas. I won't be

waiting for help, I'll be typing
"Now is the time for all good men,"
my knees tucked tightly
into the little space that's perfect
for a child playing hide-and-seek.

THE SENTENCE

"I could mess around in sentences for days."
—Scott Wrobel

It could have been a desert,
as beautiful and dry
as grammar, the sun burning
with the logic of parts of speech.
I crawled happily there, the sand of syntax

cradling my knees, rocks,
those punctuation marks, slowing me
into attentiveness. Some words tufted
like cactus, with little flowers
of sound topping them.

I lay in their shadow, cooled,
every subordinate clause
a ravine to skid down into,
dunes rising and falling
rhythmically, phrase after phrase,

an eros of contours. And when the sun
was setting on what had been written
and the shadows of letters lengthened,
verbs chased each other, desert animals,
the only motion to be seen.

Then darkness, a great, overarching full stop,
left me alone and forlorn,
waiting for the sun to rise
on the presumption
of the next sentence's opening gesture.

TEACHING FAY TO READ

We make stepping stones
of words across the floor,
across the river. Miss
a word and fall in.
Dad. No. Top. Stop.

One word and
one word and one
word will take us
from here to there.
But I want to dive off

these words and swim
in another world. Then
I couldn't say anything
without lying. Maybe the water
will lap the stones,

wet them to a shine
that speaks the silence.
Tomorrow will be sentences,
followed by whole paragraphs,
books: better start now

to wash them down.
Stand with one
foot on rock, one
on the wonderful floor
of a wave.

WASHING HIS SON'S FEET

No, he's not a baby,
he's 38 and sitting on my couch
in such a way I can see
the bottoms of his feet
and their seriously black accumulation.

Despite the social situation—
four of us, including his sister
and a friend of mine—and without
saying anything, I rise and go prepare
a plastic dishpan of soapy water,

then return to kneel like a supplicant
before him, who continues the conversation
as if I were not there sponging off each foot,
which I hold in one hand as I scrub
with the other, feeling the heft of what

has taken him so far already. And now
I remember how Mary, sister of Lazarus,
washed the feet of Jesus and dried them
with her long hair, though mine is in fact
so non-existent at my age I must

towel Austin's dry, thinking as I do
how good fortune sometimes comes
in the form of a son's dirty feet,
which, without embarrassment, thanks
to a good excuse, I can hold once again.

THE PRESENT

Hour and minute,
Emmett tells the time now,
is proud to (why not?),
so wants for his seventh
birthday a watch

(with second hand, to see
time speed) to wear
on his wrist.
It will be
obscene there,

fat as a burgher,
such a jolly
circle eating
and eating, and his wrist
so thin a tick

too loud could
(I swear) break it.
No, he will not
have that kissing-close
companion from me—

though if I brought
him into time (to be)
it must be something
to bless. Here
then (tick). Oh yes.

SUBWAY SERVICES

It used to be the Church
of the Blessed Sacrament,
at the end of my block
in childhood. Now it's the Church
of the New York City Subway,

all those parishioners
so holy they don't know it.
I like how the pews
face each other,
each rider both congregation

and celebrant. Because
communion's a visual one—
"Up to a three-second stare
is permissible but more
is intrusive, rude"—

lower your eyes as you did
before the lifted host.
"In the name of the express train
and of the local and of . . ."
The station's platform

as vestibule; the Manhattan
Transit Authority as Rome.
The message on the loudspeaker
is so unintelligible it's
the equivalent of the Latin mass.

ROSARY

So many mad ants
forming a loop, my childhood's
black border.
This is all about fingertips,
how a god can be held thus.

No, a lariat to twirl
at a religious rodeo,
lovers' toy for tying wrists,
found objet d'art to drape
over Duchamps' urinal.

If a garden of roses,
ones blackened by fire.
The small sound of the beads
falling upon themselves:
a percussion of snake vertebrae.

My aunt's and my sister's
device for navigating
their convents' dark halls;
six-shooter slung from the belt
of every Mother Superior.

The crucifix at one end
is like a river's source
to which the river returns.
Hand-warmer in the casket.
Girdle abandoned by a bride.

THE HAIRCUT

We wake in the chair
to discover the gods
are cutting our hair again
with their silver shears,
shaping our heads

to their liking. The bright tool
darts around us like lightning,
flashes to show for a second
one loss, then another,
which collect at the center

in secret—electric mound
of red brown black blonde,
autumn leafpile for children
to dive into from the height
of their old age.

The barber-gods love
their work, you can tell,
from the way they snap
the great white bib clean
before they fasten it

around our necks,
a field of snow that breaks
into waves while the stripes
on the pole outside rise higher
and higher where they cannot go.

THE STALAGMITE

"His career was a stalagmite of refusals."
—Frances Fitzgerald on Ngo Dinh Diem,
Fire in the Lake

With every no of mine,
the growth on the floor
of the cave says yes
to itself and rises
a little higher.

The bats here in what I call my life
become these words
navigating the dark,
and you are with me
in the form of water

that runs down the sides of cold rocks
and glistens.
I am rising now
to the ceiling
where I am about to kiss

a stalactite
that lowers itself
each time I weaken
and give in,
though I hardly assent;

rather, I say no
to another no.
The air trembles
between the two tips.
Kissing myself so, I will die.

STAYING THIN

What it comes down to
is this:
a line.
You are that line.
You can

sign yourself on it,
giving away your life,
or you can walk it,
performing an act
high above the crowd.

It is a matter of passage:
to go through the eye
of a needle,
to slip into the
toughest locks.

And there is always
the old-time movie
you are trapped in:
at the height of the chase
you turn sideways

and thousands of policemen,
of friends, of lovers,
race past you,
thinking you are only the sign
of a man.

ON DONATING HIS BODY TO
THE UNIVERSITY OF MINNESOTA
MEDICAL SCHOOL

I worked with students for decades.
Why not continue
after my death?
But this time, no assignments,
no papers to grade.

I'll call the class to attention
with my silent entry,
smooth and horizontal.
No roll call
in the tiered hall.

After the saw bites like a thought
I've avoided for years,
let the rose of my brain
open and open,
a rose of lessoning

all lucid at the touch
and irresistible press
of a shiny point,
the intimacy so fine
everyone gets an A.

And I hear that medical students
like to give the donations
nicknames. I'm hoping
mine is one
I can live with.

THE PERFORMANCE

We are all sacrifices
to the sun god.
My grown children say,
"You first, Daddy, you first."
An old man,

I stand on the lip
of an active volcano,
its fire licking my feet,
as if I were at
the neighborhood pool

and they
no higher than my knees.
It's my time now to
show them how
to do it, to execute

a spectacular dive,
arms out,
the body at home
in air, in smoke,
loving the fall

through the ascending
thermal drafts,
so that my children
can only
ooh and aah.

REQUEST

Bury me in a dictionary.
I'll take comfort from all the
etymological roots
twining around me,
holding me as a mother might.

Maybe near the word "assuage,"
which will assuage me,
its soft contours like plush.
Or my cousin "smithereens,"
both of us derived from Ireland.

A big dictionary,
at least the size of the
American Heritage 4th edition.
A paginated coffin,
solid and squared off.

So many words the repositories
of the human spirit, each
with its little sail
catching puffs of speech,
and I riding in those boats forever.

That such thin pages
could add up to such weight!
Like the dead,
so little to them,
so omnipresent, our very air.

HONEY: A CODA

... the Mother of Sorrows yields
to the time-weary petitioner, pouring
an answer that spreads, thickly, slowly,
a smothering and final goodness,
over an entire life.
                    —from the author's "Honey"

The mourners one by one pause
before her little compartment,
its roof raised,
to dip a fingertip
not into holy water

but into the sweet glaze
on every surface therein
from plush to skin—
the youngest great-niece
scolded for trying

to swim her whole hand
into the treat—
and with the finger capped
so glossily,
threatening to drip,

make no sign of the cross
but rather, as they
turn away, carry the finger up
into the mouth and marvel,
making restrained

but audible sounds
of appreciation
at the Grade A quality
until they suck and suck
their fingertips clean.

ABOUT THE AUTHOR

Philip Dacey is the author of eleven previous books of poetry, most recently *Mosquito Operas: New and Selected Short Poems* (Rain Mountain Press, 2010) and *Vertebrae Rosaries: 50 Sonnets* (Red Dragonfly Press, 2009). The winner of three Pushcart Prizes, he has written entire collections about Gerard Manley Hopkins, Thomas Eakins, and New York City. His other awards include a Discovery Award from the New York YM-YWHA's Poetry Center and various fellowships (a Fulbright to Yugoslavia, a Woodrow Wilson to Stanford, and two in creative writing from the National Endowment for the Arts). His work has appeared in such leading periodicals as *The Nation, Hudson Review, Poetry, The Southern Review, The Paris Review, Partisan Review, The New York Times, American Review, The American Poetry Review,* and *The Georgia Review.* With David Jauss, he co-edited *Strong Measures: Contemporary American Poetry in Traditional Forms* (Harper & Row, 1986). After an eight-year post-retirement adventure as a resident of Manhattan's Upper West Side, he returned in 2012 to Minnesota, where he taught for 35 years at Southwest Minnesota State University, in Marshall, to live in Minneapolis in the Lakes District with his partner, Alixa Doom.

Printed in the United States of America

www.ingramcontent.com/pod-product-compliance
Lightning Source LLC
Chambersburg PA
CBHW032029090426
42741CB00006B/791